All Things BRIGHT and BEAUTIFUL

Illustrated by
Jean Claude

Lyrics by
Cecil Frances Alexander

All things bright and beautiful,
All creatures great and small,

All things wise and wonderful,
The Lord God made them all.

Each little flower that opens,

Each little bird that sings,

He made their glowing colors,

He made their tiny wings.

All things bright and beautiful.
All creatures great and small,
All things wise and wonderful,
The Lord God made them all.

The purple-headed mountains,
The river running by,

The sunset, and the morning,
That brightens up the sky.

All things bright and beautiful,
All creatures great and small,

All things wise and wonderful,
The Lord God made them all.

The cold wind in the winter,

The pleasant summer sun,

He made them
every one.

All things bright and beautiful,
All creatures great and small,

All things wise and wonderful,
The Lord God made them all.

The tall trees in the greenwood,
The meadows where we play.

The rushes by the water,
We gather every day.

All things bright and beautiful,
All creatures great and small,

All things wise and wonderful,
The Lord God made them all.

He gave us eyes to see them,
And lips that we might tell
How great is God Almighty,
Who has made all things well.

All things bright and beautiful,
All creatures great and small,

All things wise and wonderful,
The Lord God made them all.

Cecil Frances Alexander was born in 1818 in Dublin. She was an acclaimed poet and writer of hymns, including the popular "All things bright and beautiful," "Once in royal David's city" and "There is a green hill far away." She married in 1850 and was actively involved in many charities, including founding a school for the deaf.

Illustrations copyright © 2019 Jean Claude

Published by Kregel Children's, an imprint of Kregel Publications, 2450 Oak Industrial Dr. NE, Grand Rapids, Michigan 49505 USA under special arrangement with the Society for Promoting Christian Knowledge, London, England.

Original edition published in English under the title *All Things Bright and Beautiful* by the Society for Promoting Christian Knowledge, London, England. All rights reserved.

A catalog record for this book is available from the British Library.

ISBN 978-0-8254-4765-5

Printed in Hong Kong